CW00376928

Independently Published 2021

Clipart prints © bookbildr

Photographs © E S Monk

ISBN 9798713170370

Healed By My Horses

Memoir

By

E.S. Monk

Healed By My Horses

For Mum

Together we withstood the storm

And

For my horses.

Introduction

Cira

Cira was born on the first of May 2014 and came to me in April 2015 when she was eleven months old.

She was found, along with other foals, locked inside a stable knee-deep in her own filth. She was emaciated, her little baby bones protruding through her foal fluff, and she was terrified.

Not what you would call an ideal first horse! I'd had a few riding lessons as a child, a few more in my early twenties, and by the time I turned thirty I decided it was time to get my own horse. The search for my new best friend began.

I saw the advert: black, cob filly, to make 14.2. Absolutely not what I was looking for. My criteria were bombproof happy hacker and safe around young children. What was I thinking when I paused over the advert? Needless to say, I lost all of my senses and enquired.

The reply came. It was a very honest reply, explaining what had happened to her and how she had been found, and it included a picture.

As soon as I saw the frightened little creature in that photograph, I knew she and I were meant to be together. We had a long journey ahead of us, but we would get there, one day at a time.

Little Filly

Come here, little filly,

Don't be afraid.

My hands are gentle,

Only soft touches made.

You're safe, little filly,

My thoughts are kind.

Only affection

Is on my mind.

My dear little filly,

What have they done?

Locking you away,

With nowhere to run.

You're free, little filly,

It's time to move on.

The horrors you faced,

Now long gone.

Years by little filly,

How big you've grown.

Your willing heart,

The time has shown.

Come here, little filly,

My beautiful mare.

What a wonderful life,

Together we share.

Candy

Candy came to me on the first of May 2018. Candy's previous life could not have been more different from Cira's. She had lived and worked at a riding school until she was in her mid-teens, and then she became a family pony. She was loved, cared for and adored by all the family.

She was twenty when she arrived, a little arthritic but full of character and ready to join my herd alongside Cira and my little donkey, Micks.

Again, she was not really what I was looking for at the time. I was idly thinking about getting the boys a pony. Truth be told, it was more of a dream than a reality, I had many months ahead of me training my now wilful, three-year-old Cira!

Just like before, I paused when I saw her advert, but this time I didn't give in. However, the next day a friend of mine said she had seen an ideal pony for me and the boys, and asked if she should send the advert over? Well, it doesn't hurt to window shop! What are the chances? It was the same pony I had paused over the previous day. I happened to mention this to Mum, who told me she knew the address -the pony was kept two minutes down the road from her. I decided it was more than a coincidence and that I must make enquiries about this horse. The moment I sat on her for our first ride, I knew she and I were going to be great friends. A week later, she was in my paddock.

Twilight Years

My darling friend,

You have carried me for many a mile.

We have idled down those country lanes,

And watched the springtime flowers

Dancing in the breeze.

We have run, hard and fast,

Under blue skies and sunshine

Across those summer meadows.

We have clip-clopped,

Through the autumn mist

With falling leaves crunching underfoot.

Alas, winter is now upon us.

The icy wind has weakened us

And brought a chill to our bones.

My darling friend

Our twilight years have come.

As you rest your head upon my shoulder

And I wrap my arms around you

I feel your warmth from within.

My darling friend

You carried me for many a mile.

You carry me still.

My Story

On the fifth of July, 2018, my life changed forever. I can never be the same person I was before that time. I was thirty-three years old and my boys were aged six and four when I got the phone call no wife ever wants to receive. My husband had been in a serious accident with his tractor and had been airlifted to hospital.

He had suffered traumatic brain injuries and was put into an induced coma with the hope of preventing his brain from swelling. He was in intensive care for two weeks, the longest two weeks of my life.

I found the doctors to be non-committal and very vague during this time. They didn't know for sure if he would even wake up and, if he did, they couldn't say what the extent his injuries would be. Would he walk again, talk again or even know who I was?

Once he did wake up, he couldn't do any of those things. He was moved to the neurological ward for the doctors to oversee and support him whilst he learned how to do all those things again; such basic things that we naturally take for granted.

Whilst he was in the hospital, I found a lump. This was the start of a never-ending series of doctors and hospital appointments for me over the next two and a half years.

The day my husband was discharged from hospital was the day I was diagnosed with a rare, aggressive type of cancer. He came home from hospital and I went in.

Being given a cancer diagnosis is almost like being invited into a private club, a club that you have neither the inclination nor the desire to join.

The door has been held open and you have been rudely shoved through it and signed up there and then. There is no going back.

You then hop on the cancer carousel and your whole life revolves around hospital appointments and the frustrating interim period between tests and results. My treatment plan was mapped out for me from the beginning. Surgery, six rounds of chemotherapy over five months and fifteen rounds of radiotherapy over three weeks. If that all went to plan, eighteen months of preventative treatment was to follow. It was a lot to take in, yet after this bombshell was dropped on me, another tragedy shortly followed.

After my first round of chemotherapy, my dad suffered a stroke that resulted in the right side of his body being paralysed. Three weeks later, after my second round of chemotherapy, the hospital rang. Dad had taken a turn for the worse and Mum and I were advised to get there as soon as possible. Over the next twenty-four hours, we held his hands and watched as he slipped away. He left us on the thirtieth of December, 2018.

I was very close to my dad and completely adored him. To lose him during such a low point of my life was devastating beyond belief.

My husband has since made a full recovery and even the doctors were amazed at how well he recovered after such a traumatic accident. Unfortunately, after I finished chemotherapy and radiotherapy, it was clear that after our series of unfortunate events it was all simply too much. In order to process and heal from our tragic ordeals, we decided to part ways. We had to embark on the next stages of our journeys alone. It was a heart-breaking decision but we both knew it was the right thing to do. We have now been able to move forward and are content following our own paths.

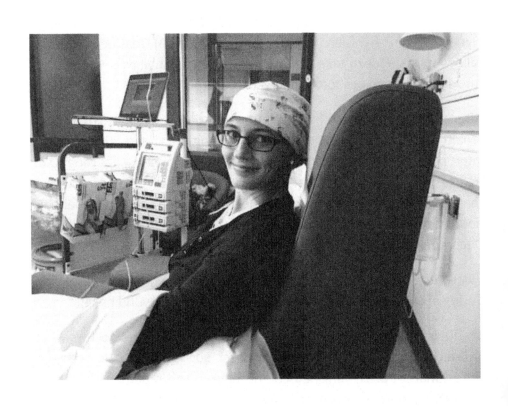

Innocence

You were like two lilies,

Floating atop the placid lake.

Basking warm glow

From sun-kissed rays.

The dark clouds of thunder

Did not caution.

The ravage waves,

Set to spill upon your pool.

The apple tree,

Under the lily pads lie,

Did shake whence thunder struck.

Though deep roots did not rumble.

Brutality of imminence

As earthly chaos reigns.

Both narrow brooks

And sacred lands impinged.

The storm held rage,

Four times the solstice.

Stealing the shadows,

Those little lilies.

Unheralded reprieve

Brought the footprints of Iris.

A sweet release,

Let tears from the bark.

The moon came full,

Not once but twice.

The pink buds of blossom

Timid with grace.

Unfolding from the squall,

The lilies of fortitude.

To bask once more

Those sun-kissed rays.

1

I have always loved animals, all of them! Big ones, small ones and of course, the fluffy cuddly ones. When I was little, my parents gave me a dolls' house. However, the dolls were swiftly removed and were never to be seen again. Instead, the house was filled with animal families and my tea parties were for my animal friends.

Our world is a wonderful place, filled with different cultures, beliefs, habitats and the most amazing wildlife. Exploring new places is a great love of mine. On my travels I have been lucky enough to combine both of my passions, experiencing new places at the same time as seeing all sorts of beautiful and exotic animals.

I have led a very privileged life with regards to exploring, adventuring and globe-trotting. My dad was a master mariner, a Captain in the Merchant Navy, and I spent all my childhood holidays travelling the world with him on board merchant navy ships. I will always be grateful for the unusual and remarkable childhood he gave me.

I was sixteen when Dad retired from life at sea but my parents, living the life they had led, always encouraged and supported me with my passion for travelling.

Dad had lived in Australia for a few years during his twenties and for my twenty-first birthday, my parents gave me flight tickets to Hong Kong and Australia so I could travel to the lands my dad had loved so much, all those years ago. Kangaroos, koalas, emus and clown fish...paradise!

When I was twenty-four, a friend and I went backpacking around South East Asia. Not content to hear all about it when I got home, my adventure-seeking, free-spirited dad flew out to Thailand to meet up with us. We had the most wonderful time together, living the backpacker dream with my dad showing us how it should be done!

The time with him went all too quickly, and it wasn't long before we had to say our goodbyes and wave each other off at the airport. Cambodia was the next adventure for us, and back to rainy old England for Dad!

After the life my parents had given me, filled with freedom and independence, you can imagine how devastating it was to lose my beloved father, the man who had nurtured and helped develop my love of life and all things in it.

The cancer diagnosis ended my independence, and my spirit was no longer free to wander. I was stuck within my grief and enclosed inside a broken body, a body that sometimes I couldn't even move. The brain fog, the nausea and the pain all led to being trapped. My wings had been clipped and I felt like a caged bird that could no longer sing.

I suffer side effects from my treatment, fatigue being the most prominent, but I was determined not to let it hold me back. My restless soul demanded freedom, so as soon as I felt able to manage the journey, twelve months after I finished chemotherapy, I went to Nepal for three weeks.

In Nepal, I travelled south to Chitwan, an animal lovers' haven. I went on safari and saw Asian rhinos running wild and free, just as they ought to be. I also saw beautiful birds, wild crocodiles swimming alongside the canoes as we paddled down the river and a lucky sighting of a gorgeous little creature, a sloth bear. It was truly an extraordinary experience.

My trip ended in Kathamandu and after exploring the city I felt I needed an animal fix. I then made the big mistake of visiting the local zoo. After seeing the animals roaming their natural habitat in Chitwan, it almost broke me to see these beautiful creatures caged and locked behind bars.

It affected me so much because I now knew what it felt like to be trapped and reliant on others to ensure my basic needs and comfort were met. Having your independence and freedom taken away from you is devastating and these animals exist like that, every single day.

This turned my thoughts to Cira. It broke my heart to think that my beautiful horse had first-hand experience of this. Due to the cruelty of a human, she did not have her basic needs met because they deliberately chose not to care for her. That barbaric attitude caused her pain and needless suffering.

During my first year of cancer treatment, I fell into some very dark times. This poem originates from my time in Nepal in a literal sense and reflects my feelings towards Cira's start in life. It is also a metaphorical depiction of how I felt during the darkest times of my treatment and grief.

To Be Free

The sun rises and the sun sets,

For those existing on the other side.

The chains around them weigh heavy,

And they weep, they weep private, silent tears.

They look out to a world full of wonder and intrigue,

A place they will never know.

As they contemplate the sun, the moon and the stars,

They watch you, watching them.

As Helios completes his journey,

Their bodies become listless,

The everlasting existence without wings,

Finally, ends.

Those grounded souls, their time has come.

Their life here, was no life at all,

With the shackles on their earthly bodies gone,

They are free.

2

Mythology has been an interest of mine for many years. I love the idea of magical and mystical lands and I let my vivid imagination run wild thinking about what life could have been like thousands of years ago.

Curled up on my sofa, with the log fire roaring, the wind howling outside, and rain hammering on the windows, surrounded by books, is one of my favourite places to be. I am transported to a world filled with gods, goddesses and mythical beasts.

Knowing this, a very good friend of mine told me about the Red Thread of Fate.

The Red Thread of Fate is an ancient tale, originally from East Asian Mythology. It centres around a belief that fate chooses, for each of us, one true love. It does not matter where you come from; the hand of fate is dealt, and at some point during your lifetime, fate will guide you towards finding your love.

The red thread is an invisible cord, tied between you and your true love, most commonly thought to be tied to your little finger. This thread can twist and bend during the trials of life, but it can never be broken. One way or another, you will meet.

When our souls are created, fate decides who will be tied to whom, even before we are born. Our life's destiny has already been decided by the time we are given breath on this earth.

I love this fable and my friend and I have discussed it many times. We talked about who could be tied to the other end of our red thread. Had we met them yet? Would we ever meet them? It all made for good old girly gossip!

As time went on and I thought back over the years, especially the recent years of my cancer journey and grief, I came to realise who had been there with me. Who was it who had been there, day in and day out, religiously offering support, kindness and a reason to get up in the morning?

It dawned on me that people come and go in our lives. Some are with us for a very short time and others walk alongside us for much longer. Only fate knows how long we will spend with the people in our lives. I believe that people come into our lives for a reason. Some are there for us to help them, others for them to help us and when a true friendship is formed, we help each other.

I realised, with a stark reality, that it wasn't a man who I wanted to be tied to the other end of my red thread. The truth of it is that my most faithful, trusted friends were my horses.

For this poem, I enjoyed letting my imagination run away with the Tale of the Red Thread to honour the never-wavering loyalty that my horses have given me. During my hours of need, it was them who gave me hope, whilst they carried me.

Our Red Thread

During a time of myths and legends,

There was once a fable told.

Where the fates decided,

How our story would unfold.

Before even the beginning had begun,

Our souls were destined forever to be,

With an invisible red thread,

Tied between you and me.

This red thread can never be broken.

It can twist and stretch and bend,

But, ultimately,

We will be together in the end.

When hearing this fable told,

I knew it to be true.

When the time was right,

I would be guided to you.

When that time came,

It was so out of place.

I looked across the paddock

And saw your kind eye and gentle face.

What luck bechanced me.

The beautiful horse I saw ahead

Was tied to the other end,

Of my invisible red thread.

3

Oxford dictionary definition.

Soul - The spiritual or immortal element in a person.

Fate - A power thought to control all events; a person's destiny.

Destiny - Fate; one's future destined by fate.

Coincidence - The chance occurrence of events which are similar or interrelate to affect developments.

I believe Candy and Cira were meant to come into my life. As explained earlier, neither of them was what I thought I was looking for, yet somehow, they entered my life. I know they are with me for a purpose and that our souls and our personalities are meant to be together. You could call it fate, destiny or just coincidence. It doesn't matter what label is used - all that matters is that we found each other.

Candy was sent to me to support and carry me through the most difficult time in my life, to help me face my demons and make it through to the other side. I truly believe that she will be with me, every step of the way.

Cira is here to offer me hope for the future and all the opportunities that will come with it. Together we will work hard and together we will reap the rewards.

Our three souls are joined, to live a life together, as best we can, during our time here on earth. My life has been made undeniably richer by having these two beautiful horses - friends - in it.

Our Soul

The seasons changed,

Before I knew

Why you had come,

And what you would do.

Time was not easy,

Right from the start.

You waited patiently,

For me to open my heart.

I was somewhat guarded,

To give you my trust.

But, over and over

You showed that I must.

You proved yourself.

Time and again,

That you could protect,

My fragile frame.

You had no doubt,

You knew all along,

That standing beside you,

Is where I belong.

My loyal friend,

You shared my pain,

Even though,

You had nothing to gain.

I hope you now know,

That I learned what you do.

When you need me,

I can also carry you.

We each are one half

Of our spirited soul.

When I met you

We became whole.

4

Cira was gently backed at three and half by one of my good friends who is a horse trainer. She was turned away over the winter and then, come spring, after her fourth birthday the time came for her to go back to school. It was such a wonderful feeling, riding my own horse, albeit under the watchful eye of my experienced friend. Green horse and novice rider, we all know how that turns out!

It had taken me two and a half years to sit on my once feral, terrified foal. Then it took another six months for her to start her actual career as my riding horse. And then my cancer diagnosis came. The surgery, chemotherapy and radiation therapy left me so weak that I often couldn't even get out of bed.

Riding a green, young horse was totally out of the question for me. That was another devastating blow. All those years of hard work and dedication, taken away from me because I was too weak to ride her.

Hindsight is a wonderful thing because looking back, the extra time off gave her the chance to be a young horse, to play and to mature. When I was finally able to manage her, she was much more level-headed and sensible, and ready for her training to begin again with my friend and for our riding lessons to start.

This is where Candy came into her own. Unlike Cira, a hardy cob who lives off fresh air and literally enjoys dancing in the rain, Candy, being an older girl, needs extra attention.

I knew that I had to do what was right for my horse, and that she had a special need for extra attention. And it was that knowledge that gave me the strength to crawl up to the yard every day that I could. Because I had to, for Candy. She doesn't keep her weight on very well, so she needs a hard feed every day, and she also needs to be rugged over the winter months. I knew that no one could look after her like I would. One of the most enjoyable things about being a horse owner is learning all the little things that your own horse likes and dislikes, and what makes them an individual.

Caring for her gave me a reason to force myself out of bed and on to the yard. As time went on, I realised that when I was with her, I felt better, even if only for a little while. Being around my horses and doing the daily yard chores made me feel a little like my old self again. Being with them, resting my head on their large shoulders, wrapping my arms around them and smelling that delicious horsey smell; in those moments, I felt at peace.

The days that I could physically pick up a saddle, I would ride her. Not for very far and not for very long, but I was free. Riding Candy meant that I could go further than I could manage walking on my own two feet. I use the term 'riding' loosely; in reality, I did no such thing. I slowly climbed, inelegantly, onto her back and sat on her. She did all the work. I was just a passenger. She kept a steady pace as we plodded along, breathing in the fresh air and enjoying the countryside views. Riding her, being with her, was my tonic, my little bit of healing for that short time.

Candy is an opinionated, bossy head mare in our little herd. Cira and I worked out very early on that our lives would go much more smoothly if Candy was allowed to lead the way.

Over the years, Candy and I have most definitely had our moments. I have loudly voiced my opinions (to no avail!) and I swear to the gods above, I can hear that horse swearing right back at me.

This is Candy's character and why I adore her so much. I love it that she feels that she has the freedom to voice her opinions, and that she knows she will always be heard. I wouldn't change my little drama queen for all the horses in the world.

When the time came, when it mattered the most, she was there for me. She knew that I was weak and unwell. She knew that what I needed was for her to be my friend and my confidante, and she instinctively knew how to behave around me to keep me safe.

I like to think that our relationship, our friendship, enables her to feel that she can share both sides of her personality with me. Over time we have learned when we both want to play and prove that our own opinion is the right one! We also both know when the other needs a softer, more gentle approach, because - well, because we're just having a bad day.

Even now I have days when I am too exhausted to ride, but it doesn't matter. I have accepted my physical capabilities now and appreciate the time I spend with my horses, whatever we are doing. The horses are turned out all day, every day, all year round, so they are able to get plenty of exercise. The days that I can ride, we do and the days that I can't, we don't.

This poem is a reflection of the hopes and dreams I once had, which were then crushed with the trials and tribulations that life put in my path.

The Linden's Mockingbird

The mockingbird weeps,

Atop her Linden tree.

Those idle thoughts

Of youth mistook.

Notes of sorrow ring,

Across that flowery meadow.

A place whence dreams

Bethought of truth.

Harsh candour of age;

No Baucis did succumb,

Nor regard her Philemon.

Like those of epics old.

She knows no oak,

Hears her melancholy tune.

Thus, tears she keeps

Within her Linden, alone.

5

I live in fear every day. That's what trauma does to you. It's the fear of losing another loved one and fear that the cancer is going to come back. The first time I was ignorant to what lay ahead of me and quite frankly, ignorance was bliss regarding the cancer treatment that I was put through. Now knowing what I would have to face, I don't think I could do it again. Many of my TNBC (triple-negative breast cancer) fellow pink ladies have had to endure the gruelling treatment for a second time and I don't think the fear of my cancer returning will ever leave me.

When I was first diagnosed, one of my lovely friends gave me the book, *Dear Cancer* by Victoria Derbyshire. Victoria survived her cancer journey, so this was a glimmer of positivity during those early days when my outlook was very negative.

However, one part of her story talks about when she wrote letters to her children in case she didn't survive. This is something I could not do. The thought of leaving my two little boys behind, motherless, made my heart break. It gave me a fear so deep that it drove me to fight as hard as I could to win my battle against this evil disease.

Losing Dad and my husband's near fatal-accident made death a reality for me. It can happen to anyone at any time. You don't have to suffer a terrible disease to die. People die every day. Young people, old people - all of us will at some point die.

Yes, during my dark times I thought about death a lot. The problem with loving someone so much is that when you face the reality of losing them, you will inevitably suffer real heartache.

I took my dad for granted. I thought he would always be with me, to guide me, help me and advise me. I have always been close to both of my parents, enjoying their company and their never-ending supply of support when it was needed. Dad has been such a huge part of my life and I will forever hold on to the memories that I have of him.

This leads to my second biggest fear... what if I lose my horses? What if I survive this godforsaken journey and I finally make it through to the other side, but I lose one of my soul mates? My horses were the ones who got me through it. They have been the emotional support that I have relied on for so long. Who would look after me and offer me the comfort I need if they were to be taken from me?

This is especially true of Candy. She has been my rock throughout my treatment - she was, and still is, there for me every step of the way. Grief and depression do funny things to you. I know now that I have support from my family and friends, but at the time, I felt like a broken record. That's the problem with cancer - it goes on and on and on. You feel like it's all old news and you don't want to continually complain about how awful everything is. Of course, my friends didn't mind. They wanted to be there to support me. It was me who didn't want to keep off-loading all of my problems on to them.

Candy was different, though. She allowed me to be myself. That's the thing with horses - they can see right through you, so there is no point in trying to pretend any different when you're around them.

Candy suffers quite badly with her arthritis now. She has to be turned out twenty-four hours a day, seven days a week. If she is stabled, she gets stiff and her arthritis gets worse. She needs very gentle exercise to loosen up her joints. I feel that we can relate to each other; our spirits are willing but our bodies are broken.

When we go for our little plods, I feel like we are two little old ladies, just a pair of friends, out and about, putting the world to rights. We like to talk about how things used to be.

When Candy first came to me, we would fly like the wind. She loved to run, and I loved going along for the ride. She was the perfect horse. She never took it upon herself to take off whenever it suited her - that sort of behaviour would have been beneath her! She asked, politely. I could just feel her and knew what she wanted. All it took was the most gentle squeeze from me and that was her cue...we were gone! I felt no fear with her, I would let her go and she made me fly. The freedom and the exhilaration when you have a horse that can do that for you gives you the most amazing feeling. I would give the gentlest squeeze on her reins, and she would ask, "Are you sure you want to slow down? We're having so much fun!" Then, depending on circumstances, she would slow, or if I felt her decision was the better one, we continued to run, together.

We can't run together anymore - her joints are too stiff now. But it doesn't matter. We plod, we talk, we enjoy each other's company and that is enough.

The fear of losing her plagued me with anxiety and plunged me even deeper into my depression. The thought of losing my best friend and my confidante left me in my ever-darkening place for a long time.

I wrote this poem to try and control and contain my depressive, negative thought process about the possibility of losing one of my horses. Logically, we are all going to cross that rainbow bridge at some point and all we can do is love and care for our horses, to the best of our ability, whilst they are with us.

Unfortunately, when one is in the depths of darkness, logic is difficult to grasp. I already had plenty to feel miserable about so why I decided to add this to the list is beyond me! I think I felt that my horses were my small ray of hope in what was a very wretched existence, and maybe if I were to lose one, that would also be the loss of my hope.

I found that writing this poem helped me to process all the things that were going on around me which I couldn't control.

Forever

You are old now,

A little bit broken.

Although, those words

Need not be spoken.

We used to run,

Together, you and I.

Your speed and grace,

Allowed us to fly.

Long years can't escape,

Aches and pain.

A heavy heart watches,

Days you are lame.

I still love you,

Like I always did.

Even now, you have

So much to give.

The little things

Are still the same.

You sleep so peacefully

When brushing your mane.

Time is not wasted,

Watching you graze.

Your shimmering coat

In summer's day haze.

No longer a thought,

What we used to do.

All that matters

Is I still have you.

Today and every day,

Together, you and me.

My darling horse,

You will forever be.

6

A cancer diagnosis is like a package deal for depression. First of all, they talk to you in percentages. If you have x treatment plus y treatment plus z treatment, you have...% chance of surviving. That conversation with your oncologist is never a fun one! First, you have to deal with your initial diagnosis, tests, tests and more tests, so they can work out your stage/grade/percentage and then comes the joyful journey that is cancer treatment.

On top of all of that, you then have to deal with all of the physical changes that happen to your body. The first question I asked was "Will I lose my hair?" In the grand scheme of things, losing your hair to live is not such a big deal, but accepting this is easier said than done when faced with the fact that you will be bald for the best part of twelve months.

I'm very lucky to have a lovely friend who is a hairdresser and she was right by my side offering help once we knew the fate of my hair. She came over to my house to cut my (waist-length, glossy, pride and joy) hair into a bob. Once chemo started, her scissors came back out to crop my hair into a pixie style. I decided that this was one of the few things I still had some control over and that I would be the one to decided when to cut my hair, not the cancer.

Your hair starts to fall out around ten days after you start chemo, which is a surprisingly painful experience. Armed with this information, another of my lovely friends came to my aid. She gave me the most awesome headscarf I have ever seen, bright pink with little silver, sparkly unicorns on it!

My sister lives miles away from me, at the other end of the country. When she heard about my diagnosis, she sent me a parcel...Diamond earrings! She said that there was nothing anyone could do about losing my hair, but I could still look good!

Thanks to my friends and my sister I still managed to keep my own personal, quirky style throughout my treatment.

The other treat chemo delivers you is...weight gain. Yep, as if life didn't suck enough! I put on one and a half stone during my treatment, mainly from all the steroids I had to take. By the time I had finished chemo I couldn't fit into any of my clothes. Isn't cancer just a peach!

It took over two years for me to process and deal with the accident, my initial cancer diagnosis, losing my dad, undergoing all the treatment and then the final trauma - that everything that had happened resulted in the breakdown of my marriage. I was what one might call emotionally and physically broken.

Horses are now used professionally as therapy animals and many people who have suffered terrible traumas have been able to heal through Equine Assisted Therapy Programs.

Wikipedia's definition:

"Equine Assisted Therapy encompasses a range of treatments that involve activities with horses and other equines to promote human physical and mental health."

Healing does not come instantly. Trauma and devastation can all happen in a split second but dealing with the aftermath can sometimes take years to process. At times it can seem that our depression, pain and suffering know no bounds and will continue to ruthlessly haunt us.

I held on to the fact that when dawn broke, I could see my horses again and at least then, for the short time I was with them, they would bring calmness and I would feel a sense of peace.

It was my horses who slowly pieced me back together. As time went on, each time I left them, their healing magic stayed with me a little while longer. In those darkest hours, their silent, comforting warmth healed my mind and soul. They were the one constant thing for me, in a time when I had no control over all that was happening to me and around me.

I am so very privileged to have personally experienced the healing power of horses through Cira and Candy.

This poem was from the long, medically-induced nights of insomnia. This was a time when sleep eluded me, when I was so very desperate for it to release me from my never-ending sorrow.

Whispers

I close my eyes to rest my mind from the darkness that envelopes me.

I sleep to dream and dream to wake in a beautiful world around me.

Time stands still during the quiescence of the night.

Dreams do not come to ease my sorrow or heal the world around me.

I seek you out in the crisp, cold air.

Your shadow dancing in the moonlight.

I hear your gentle nicker and feel your soft, warm muzzle on my skin.

My healing has begun.

When all is quiet, throughout the twilight hours,

You speak to me.

Before dawn rises, your whispers,

They make the world beautiful around me.

As One

Let us ride, you and I

For,

When your hoof beats,

Match my heartbeat

We are one.

7

Do you ever just know things? The sort of things that once you know, you can't not know. Then you try and bury those thoughts because you could not bear it if they came true.

I knew in January 2018 that my dad was going to die that year. I don't know why or how, I just knew. Fair play to him, he held out until the thirtieth of December, but all the same, he died in 2018.

As the weeks then months slipped by, I started to relax the ugly, unwanted feeling inside me. I thought, maybe I'm wrong, please let me be wrong. Unfortunately, I wasn't.

I also knew I had cancer. Not straight away, but whilst I was waiting for my biopsy results, that dreaded feeling of mine came again. I had told my girlfriends I had found a lump. They were super supportive and positive about it all. They told me that I was young and that lots of women found lumps that turned out to be cysts or fatty tissue and I had nothing to worry about. Again, my instincts were correct.

The accident on the fifth of July, that was a shocker! That one came out of the blue as I did not see that one was coming. I guess I don't know everything!

Over the years I've become very spiritual and believe that when we die, we leave our earthly bodies behind and our spirits move on to another place. I also believe that crossed over spirits can reach out to us. They can offer us guidance and help. We just have to be open to receiving their messages.

Chemotherapy...well, what a bitch that is! There is absolutely no way to sugar coat it. Nothing and no one can prepare you for the hell on earth you face once that poison is pumped into your body. Ironic, isn't it- poison to protect you.

Your body is filled with so many drugs, you can literally feel the poison circulating around your body and there is no way to escape it. It's sort of a one-way ticket to misery and depression! You know you need to have it in order to keep yourself alive, so you reluctantly agree to get on that chemo carousel.

Being honest, I wanted out. After the first two rounds, I was broken. After each chemotherapy round, usually two weeks after the dose, one week before the next dose, you see your oncologist. It's for a sort of chit-chat to see how you're getting on.

I remember the conversation I had with my oncologist after my second round. It went along the lines of:

"I don't like it, I'd rather not do it anymore if that's ok by you? Maybe, at best, I suppose I could do it if you reduced my dosage?"

Hahaha, as if! My oncologist's reply, in a cool, calm and collected voice:

"No, your cancer is too nasty to reduce your dose, I think it's best we carry on as you are."

In typical British, non-fussing fashion...

"Oh, ok then, I guess we'll do what you want to do, round three it is. Good chat!"

The week of doom soon came around and there I was again, my pyjamas on, in bed, awaiting the misery of round three to kick in. I could feel it building. For me, it started slowly. As each hour passed, the feeling of nausea got worse and worse until it reached the point of no return. At this point, I would have gladly relinquished myself to the angel of death if he had taken it upon himself to visit me.

However, that night, someone else did. Dad came to me. I could feel his spirit all around me. I could feel him shielding me from the pain and that night, the point of no return was never reached.

Even after death, my beloved father was still being my dad, protecting me.

Dad

You can rest now.

My Horses,

They have healed me.

Secrets of the Angels

You have taken your place alongside the angels.

A place so very far away from me.

I know my life here is not yet done.

But one day I will be with you again.

Until that day comes, during my times

Of melancholy and sadness, you come to me.

You wrap your angel wings around me.

For now that you sit amongst them, you hear their whispers.

Through their soothing, gentle voices.

You know my secrets, for the angels.

Today

Let us sit,

For a little while.

And feel the warmth

Of the sun on our backs.

Let us be,

For a little while.

In this fragrant meadow

Of bumblebees and buttercups.

Let us listen,

For a little while.

The grasses rustle and the gentle trickling brook,

The music of nature's own.

Let us share,

For a little while.

This moment in time.

For memories, when days have passed.

Let us remember,

Always.

The promise of tomorrow...

A gift not always to be gifted.

So, let us walk,

For a little while.

Our footprints, side by side,

Today.

At Sea

He climbed aboard a merchant ship,

To sail to foreign lands.

He studied the charts and clasped a globe,

Between his gentle hands.

With the stars as his guide,

He plotted her course with ease.

Under the clear night sky,

He set sail for the seven seas.

From the bridge he watched,

Sextant and compass by his side,

The beauty of his ship

As through the waves, she did glide.

My dearest Captain,

This voyage, you will not return.

The ache in my heart,

Will forever burn.

8

Things are not always as they seem.

Sometimes we have to weather the storm,

To see the beauty on the other side.

The Dark Side

The fates, they have chosen

To cast a shadow all around me.

They have directed my path

To the dark side of the moon.

There is no springtime or butterflies

In the land that now envelopes me.

I am met with dark clouds and thunder

Under an ever-blackening sky.

My body is weakened

As the cold seeps into my bones.

My sorrow filled heart,

It has lost its way.

When will I find the key?

To unlock the answers,

And find my path

To the other side of the moon.

Bright side of the moon

Once upon a time,

A tale was told.

About an enchanted woodland,

Full of beauty to behold.

At the heart of this land,

Golden rays of sunshine bring light.

With robins and butterflies a plenty,

All the flowers are vibrant and bright.

This magical, mystical world,

Where the pixies and fairies call home.

It is also the place,

Where the shy, wild horses roam.

An avenue of apple trees, filled with blossom

Is the path to the bright side of the moon.

May I have the strength to leave the dark side

And find my way there soon.

I feel I have come full circle now. My time on the dark side is over and I have slowly but surely followed my path to the bright side of the moon.

Although my life will never be the same as it once was, my journey has made me a stronger person for it. I appreciate all things in life, especially the little things. On a beautiful sunny day in spring, I literally stop and smell the pretty hedgerow flowers. There is nowhere more beautiful than Cornwall in springtime. Spring is also my favourite time to ride, clip-clopping along the country lanes, enjoying my horses and the beauty that is all around us.

I have written this book with the hope of bringing comfort to those who might need it the most. To those who are in the depths of their own darkness with no sight of light ahead. I hope this will bring some welcomed relief and that, at some point in the not-too-distant future, a glimmer of light will shine through and your darkness will slowly fade away. You are not alone.

I am so very grateful for all the wonderful things in my life right now and I'm looking forward to the adventures lying ahead of me.

This photograph was taken a few weeks before the fifth of July, 2018. It was the last perfect day I had before devastation occurred. My horsey friends and I hired horses from a local riding school to go for an exhilarating blast across the moors. The weather could not have been more glorious if we had chosen it ourselves. A trip to the local pub followed for gossip and lunch. Horses, friends and good food - life doesn't get much better than that.

My horses gave me the support and comfort I needed to get me through the most difficult time of my life and helped me to deal with the traumas that had been thrown at me. They were the only ones I could let in and the only ones who could give me what I needed at the time.

But my human friends were still waiting for me. Going through three tragedies in such a short space of time showed me what loyal, caring and amazing friends I have. I include in this my horsey and non-horsey friends. Even when I felt I couldn't turn to them for help, though at times I should have, they were there, waiting for me. They were always waiting to support me when I needed them to lean on. One friend turned up religiously, every week, to walk my dog for me and if the boys were home from school, she would take them out for a treat as well. No questions asked, just there, available for me if I needed her.

The thing with cancer and grief is that it doesn't just happen to you. It affects all of your loved ones around you. They have to sit back and watch you suffer and be completely helpless about the whole situation. They can't fix you, they can't take the physical pain away from the cancer drugs and they can't bring your loved one back. They have to go through their own journey, learning how to cope with a seriously ill friend and at the same time appearing strong on the outside. Yet, on the inside, they are hurting too. No one offers them any support, it's the walking corpse in the headscarf that people feel sorry for. But it's also a trauma for them to watch their friend go through such a life-changing, devastating journey. It was even more traumatic for my mum to go through. Being a mother myself, I can imagine how horrific it must feel to watch your child suffer so greatly.

I have come through to the other side now, and guess what? My friends and I, we drink tea, we eat cake, we put the worlds to rights, and we ride, just like we always did.

Reflection

Gaze out yonder

And rest thine eyes,

Upon the untamed lands,

Those wild horses roam.

Nature's own perfection,

Their wilderness home.

Though, befall both

Trepidation and delight.

Inconsequential time.

A thought to think.

Passed deeds not dwelt

Nor the morrow regard.

A myriad of beauty,

Those momental beings.

Their sacred gift,

A quietness within.

Printed in Great Britain
by Amazon

83474368R00058